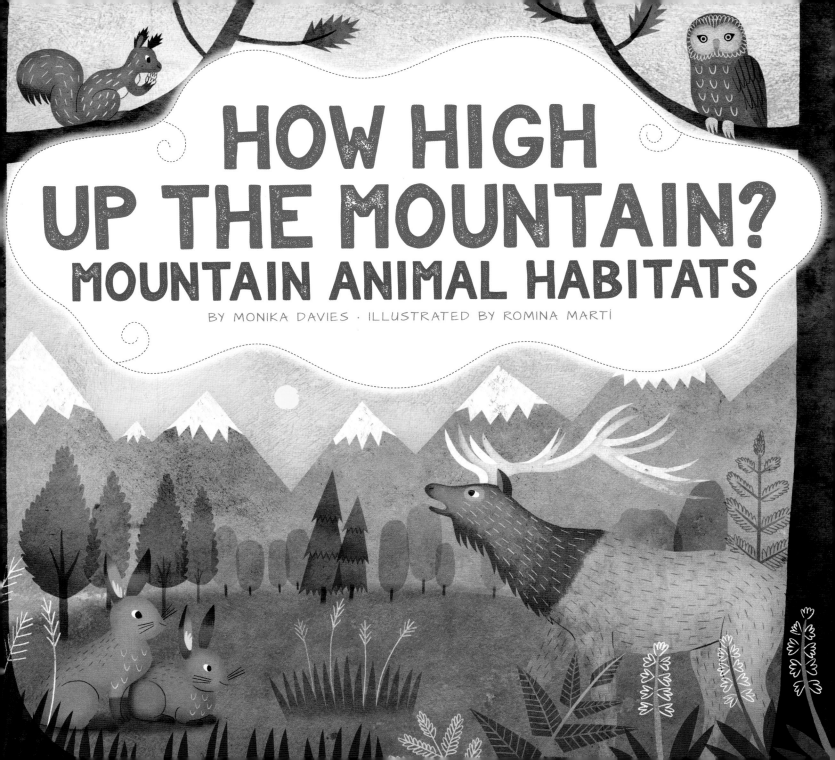

HOW HIGH UP THE MOUNTAIN?
MOUNTAIN ANIMAL HABITATS

BY MONIKA DAVIES · ILLUSTRATED BY ROMINA MARTÍ

Amicus Illustrated and Amicus Ink
are imprints of Amicus
P.O. Box 1329
Mankato, MN 56002
www.amicuspublishing.us

Library of Congress Cataloging-in-Publication Data
Names: Davies, Monika, author. | Marti, Romina, illustrator.
Title: How high up the mountain? : mountain animal habitats / by
   Monika Davies ; illustrated by Romina Marti.
Other titles: Mountain animal habitats
Description: Mankato, MN : Amicus Illustrated, [2019] | Series:
   Animals measure up | Audience: K to grade 3. | Includes
   bibliographical references.
Identifiers: LCCN 2017057985 (print) | LCCN 2017060824
   (ebook) | ISBN 9781681514710 (pdf) | ISBN 9781681513898
   (library binding) | ISBN 9781681523095 (pbk.)
Subjects: LCSH: Mountain ecology--Juvenile literature. | Mountain
   animals--Juvenile literature. | Animal behavior--Juvenile literature.
Classification: LCC QH541.5.M65 (ebook) | LCC QH541.5.M65
   D3845 2019 (print) | DDC 577.5/3--dc23
LC record available at https://lccn.loc.gov/2017057985

Editor: Rebecca Glaser
Designer: Kathleen Petelinsek

Printed in the United States of America.

HC 10 9 8 7 6 5 4 3 2 1
PB 10 9 8 7 6 5 4 3 2 1

About the Author

When she was young, Monika lived near the Canadian
Rocky Mountains. Every year, she drives through this
beautiful mountain range. Monika graduated from the
University of British Columbia with a bachelor of fine arts
in creative writing. She has written over eighteen books
for young readers.

About the Illustrator

Romina Martí is an illustrator who lives and works in
Barcelona, Spain, where her ideas come to life for all
audiences. She loves to discover and draw all kinds of
creatures from around the planet, who then become the
main characters for the majority of her work. To learn
more, go to: rominamarti.com

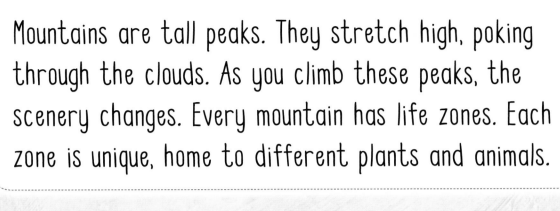

Mountains are tall peaks. They stretch high, poking through the clouds. As you climb these peaks, the scenery changes. Every mountain has life zones. Each zone is unique, home to different plants and animals.

Let's begin our hike up! Your first stop is the grasslands. This zone is 4,000 feet (1,200 m) above sea level. Here, bunchgrasses sway in the breeze. Cactuses lift prickly arms to the sun. Jackrabbits hop by. Coyotes prowl past.

6,000

5,500

5,000

4,500

4,000
FEET

1,800

1,700

1,600

1,500

1,400

1,300

1,200
METERS

5

Up you go! Soon, you reach the foothills. This life zone starts at 6,000 feet (1,800 m) high. Here, the soil is packed with gravel.

Only short shrubs and small trees can grow here. A Western scrub jay dashes about, looking for food.

Phew! You climb to 8,000 feet (2,400 meters). This is the montane zone. Here, the temperature drops. Rain and snow fall hard. Douglas firs grow in the shade. Ponderosa pines line the sunny paths. Abert's squirrels hide in the pines. These shy creatures build nests in the branches.

3,000
2,900
2,800
2,700
2,600
2,500
2,400
M

Nearby, aspen trees grow in thick crowds. Their leaves flicker in the wind.

Rocky Mountain elk live here. These elk like to graze. One of their favorite meals is aspen bark.

3,000

2,900

2,800

2,700

2,600

2,500

2,400 M

Keep going! You're now at the subalpine zone. It's 10,000 feet (3,000 meters) above sea level. Snow covers the ground for most of the year in this zone.

11,500

11,000

10,500

10,000
FT

3,500

3,400

3,300

3,200

3,100

3,000 M

This zone is wet, windy, and cold, but hardy spruce and fir trees still take root here. Plants grow close to the ground.

Who lives in the subalpine zone? Snowshoe hares sprint past. In the winter, their white coats blend into the snow. This makes it tough for predators to spot them! Hidden in the fir trees are boreal owls. These owls hunt mice under the cloak of the night.

11,500

11,000

10,500

10,000
FT

3,500

3,400

3,300

3,200

3,100

3,000
M

15

At last, you reach the peak! You're now in the alpine zone. It starts at a height of 11,500 feet (3,500 meters).

14,000

13,500

13,000

12,500

12,000

11,500
FT

This is the tundra. Here, snowstorms are common. Dry winds blow cold air in. No trees grow here. But small plants sprout briefly. In the summer, forget-me-nots bloom in blue hues.

4,200

4,100

4,000

3,900

3,800

3,700

3,600

3,500 M

14,000

13,500

13,000

12,500

12,000

11,500 FT

4,200

4,100

4,000

3,900

3,800

3,700

3,600

3,500 M

Here, tiny pikas make their home. These short-legged creatures feed on green plants. They store up plants in "haypiles" for winter. Close by, bighorn sheep climb the steep cliffs. They can scamper up high to escape from predators.

Animals and plants are well adapted to the climates of the mountain life zones. Life on the mountain is a sight to behold.

MOUNTAIN LIFE ZONES

bighorn sheep

pikas

boreal owls

snowshoe hares

Rocky Mountain elk

Abert's squirrels

Western scrub jays

jackrabbits

coyotes

GLOSSARY

bunchgrass A type of grass that grows in clumps instead of in a flat lawn.

climate The usual weather conditions in a particular place or region.

graze To eat grass or other plants that are growing in a field or pasture.

life zone A region characterized by specific plants, animals, and weather.

pika A small animal species, related to rabbits, that lives high in the mountains.

predator An animal that hunts other animals for food.

tundra Large areas of land in the Arctic and on mountaintops where there are no trees and the ground is always frozen.

READ MORE

Hinman, Bonnie. **Keystone Species that Live in the Mountains**. Hockessin, Del.: Mitchell Lane Publishers, 2016.

Howell, Izzi. **Mountain Geo Facts**. New York: Crabtree Publishing Company, 2018.

Waxman, Laura Hamilton. **Life on a Mountain**. Minneapolis: Bellwether Media, 2016.

WEBSITES

Life Zones and Habitats of New Mexico

http://www.wildlife.state.nm.us/download/education/conservation /coloring-books/Life-Zones-Coloring-Book.pdf

Dive deep into the habitats of New Mexico with this informative coloring book!

Mountain Habitats

https://kids.nationalgeographic.com/explore/nature/habitats/mountain/

View gorgeous mountain photos and read about animals that live in mountain habitats.

Rocky Mountain Animals

https://www.nps.gov/romo/learn/nature/animals.htm

Check out National Park Service's site and get to know Rocky Mountain animals.

Every effort has been made to ensure that these websites are appropriate for children. However, because of the nature of the Internet, it is impossible to guarantee that these sites will remain active indefinitely or that their contents will not be altered.